Social Networking

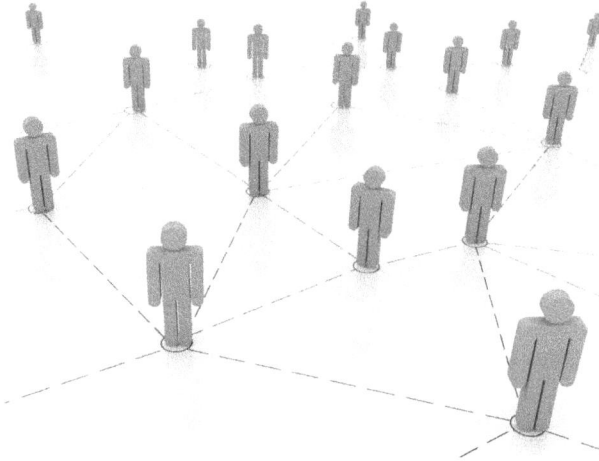

Throughout
Your Career

April M. Williams

CyberLife

© 2010 Published by AMW Inc.

CyberLife™

Contents

CyberLife™

SOCIAL NETWORKING FOR EACH STAGE OF YOUR CAREER

What's All the Buzz About?

It seems everyone is talking about social networking tools these days. Newspaper stories and daily comics make light of our "tweets". We have all heard about social networking and many of us are using these sites regularly. In fact, these tools have sparked a communication revolution by changing how we talk with each other and the speed at which information travels.

If you are a professional looking for a new job, considering a career change or even planning to be in the job market for more than one more year, it is

important to understand how to leverage the most
common social networking tools. If you are not
effectively managing your online network you will
appear out dated and behind the times to current
employers or recruiters. Currently, 80% of all
companies use LinkedIn as their primary
recruiting tool. That means if you are not using
LinkedIn effectively, other candidates will be hired
for the job, that may have been a perfect fit for you.

> *"Swim in the sea where hiring managers
> are fishing for you."* April M. Williams

Hiring managers and recruiters actively use these
sites because they are low cost and effective at
identifying good candidates. They have found there
is no need to pay for expensive ads on job search
boards when unlimited numbers of qualified
candidates are easily accessible on social
networking sites. They are fishing in a well-stocked

CyberLife

sea of potential hires. Of course, you do not have to swim in these social networking sites. If you choose to stay out, remember that you will not be where the hiring managers are looking for you.

Within this book we will cover the special considerations for using social networking tools at different career stages we may transition through over the course of our work life. Your use of the tools will be different when you are in college, employed by others or self-employed. You may even find yourself in more than one of these career stages at the same time. For example, you may be an employee at one company while at the same time, an entrepreneur running your own business. For each of these stages of your professional career, there are specific strategies you can use to make the most of social networking tools.

CyberLife

There are many different social networking tools available now and new applications appear each day. We will focus on today's most popular tools and techniques to get the biggest bang from your social networking efforts. We will cover the common features among these sites as well as what makes each site unique and a good match for your specific career stage.

You may see mention of terms unfamiliar to you. Refer to the glossary at the end of this book for more detail on these terms.

CyberLife

Common Features of Social Networking Sites

As you begin learning about social networking sites, you will find most of them have common features. When getting started with your first social networking site, you may feel overwhelmed. Take your time learning how to use the tools. As you become comfortable with the features and benefits of using these sites, you will feel more secure. The next social networking site you learn will seem easier because you will understand the basic concepts and functionality. You will find similarities between many of these sites.

Here are some of the common features you will find in most social networking sites.

CyberLife

Cost:

Almost all of the social networking applications available provide free basic services, though some sites offer premium membership with advanced functions and features. Start with the fundamental free membership and later evaluate your specific need to upgrade. For most job seekers and professionals, the basic plans provide enough performance and functionality to suit your needs. Determine your need to upgrade based on how frequently you hit the maximum use of the features included with your basic free membership.

CyberLife

Profile:

Your social networking profile is your opportunity to share information about you or your company with others. It is up to you to choose the type and amount of information you would like to share. It is common to see contact information including your name, email address, phone number and website. If you blog, include a link to your blog site here. Direct others to your preferred method of contact.

Profiles often include information about the type of business you are in or service you provide. This is where you can describe how you add value for clients or partners. You can include a link to your profile on other social networking sites. All these links are inbound hyperlinks to your other profiles and sites increasing your search engine optimization.

Connections:

Different sites have different names for the other members you are connected to including: connections, friends, followers and network. The power of your network is based upon the number of connections you have. A greater number of connections allow you to reach a wider audience with your message. When you are part of a large network, others can more easily find you.

CyberLife

Status:

The status section is where you can post a short status or update. This micro message is a way for you to market yourself by highlighting changes, news or sales messages. Your message is often restricted to 140 characters or less which requires careful thought to effectively communicate within the size constraints. Long URLs can be shortened with tools like Bit.ly (http://Bit.ly) or TinyURL (http://tinyurl.com).

CyberLife

URL Shorteners:

Long website addresses or URLs can be shortened to a few characters in length using link shortening tools like Bit.ly (http://bit.ly) or TinyURL (http://tinyurl.com). These sites create a new URL which redirects the reader to the original webpage.

Some URL shortening sites allow you to customize the new URL for readability and recognition. Entering this custom shortened URL

http://bit.ly/AprilBlogs

In your web browser will redirect you to my Wordpress blog.

P a g e | **14**

CyberLife

Tools

You cannot possibly be an expert and avid user of every one of the social networking tools available today. Even social networking experts are not experts on all of the tools. The key point to remember is to use the tools that allow you to make contact with and nurture relationships with hiring managers, strategic connections and target customers. The most important professional social networking tools today are LinkedIn, Twitter, Facebook, YouTube and blogs.

Choose Your Tools

Each of the different social networking tools draws a different audience. One of the keys to making the most of your social networking efforts is to use the appropriate tools to reach your target audience. Different people gravitate to different tools. It is more effective to reach others by using the communications tool they prefer rather than the tool you like to use.

Following is an overview of today's most popular social networking tools. In later sections of this book we will cover the specific features and functions of each tool. You will see how you can leverage these tools to achieve your goals at each stage of your career.

CyberLife

LinkedIn

For professionals who want to do business with other professionals, LinkedIn (www.linkedin.com) is the tool of choice. It is also the best tool for business to business sales. This is by far the most effective way to spend time online. Over 50 million users from over 200 countries around the world are now members. Employees from all Fortune 500 companies have profiles here. You can find members representing 170 different industries. Use this tool to build relationships with other professionals, demonstrate your expertise and as a research tool.

Log on to LinkedIn to create an online profile to highlight your skills and unique selling proposition. Your profile should let other members know what makes you special and different from your competition. Build a network of peers and

CyberLife

partners by connecting. LinkedIn becomes a more powerful networking tool as you increase the number of your connections.

Create a company page on LinkedIn and describe your products and services so others can find you. Fortune 500 companies and entrepreneurs alike can create a free company profile on LinkedIn. Link your company's website, employees and blog all to this one company page. This gives your company another inbound link for improved search engine optimization for increased visitor traffic to your website.

Search engines rank LinkedIn profiles near the top of search results. Most people find their LinkedIn profile is the first result when they search their name on Google (http://www.google.com). Readers who are searching for you are most likely to read

CyberLife

the entries which appear at the top of a search results page.

Search LinkedIn Groups and join those related to your profession, industry, outside interests, geographic location, alumni, former employer or any other passions. You can be a member of up to 50 different groups. Some groups are restricted so read the description to see if you meet the membership criteria.

Generally, it is more difficult to connect with LinkedIn members who are not directly connected to you. Group members are not connected to each other one-to-one but through the group. By joining a number of groups with large memberships you can send individual messages to other group members. Members of those groups show up in search results, as do your direct, first level connections.

CyberLife

LinkedIn's Question and Answer section is a way to quickly research a topic or poll public opinion. If there is a subject you are interested in learning more about, search the answered questions for previously answered questions. If you do not see a response that answers your specific question, ask a question of your own and let your fellow experts respond with their perspective. This is a quick and easy way to gather research data.

You can establish your expertise in your field by answering questions related to your field of interest. Search the Answers section for keywords others might use in their questions. Your answer can be short and to the point or more detailed. You can reference your comments on other websites or materials in your response.

CyberLife™

Twitter

Twitter (www.twitter.com) is the fastest growing social networking tool. You create a profile and others choose to follow you. The site is based simply on posting 140 character messages called tweets you post for your followers to read. By incorporating links and relevant keywords, members are found by others who are interested in their message.

Hashtags (#) are used to aggregate and sort messages on a topic or track a conversation. Tweets about Chicago are easily identified when they include the hashtag "#Chicago". Create your own combination of letters, numbers and characters then encourage others to tweet using this identifier to follow a discussion.

P a g e | **21**

Twitter is often used as a massive database filled with posts related to any keyword you can imagine. Rich with searchable content, it is a favorite research site for hiring managers, recruiters and customers.

Twitter is a real time communications tool. You will find the hottest news in the "Trending Topics" section on Twitter's homepage. When readers find a post they feel their audience will benefit from reading, they can retweet or rebroadcast the message to their audience. A single message can be retweeted any number of times. Interesting or entertaining posts often go viral and spread rapidly.

Twitter initially launched with a streamlined interface and limited functionality. As a result, other companies have developed tools to enhance and extend Twitter. These tools can automate and

CyberLife

simplify your experience. Recently, Twitter added additional features to make the site more useful.

Facebook

Facebook (www.facebook.com) has wide demographics compared to other social media sites. While this was once the domain of the teen scene, it is now the place where you will find young and old alike. People in all different career stages are members. The use of text, pictures, audio and video make for rich content.

Third party developers have created a variety of applications to extend Facebook's functionality. Most are safe and often useful. Beware that Facebook does not make any guarantees on these applications. On occasion, members found links they clicked on within Facebook caused computer viruses. As with any internet link, do not click on a link if you are not sure where it will lead.

Some members enjoy the many online games in Facebook; i.e. Mafia Wars and Farmville. You can challenge other members to battles of wit or just have fun. These games have an allure and while you are playing, hours will slip away without your knowledge. If you are easily lured into this type of activity, know your limits before you get started. These games can be addicting.

In addition to profile pages, you can create Fan and Group pages each designed with a different purpose. A Fan page is for public figures to broadcast information to those interested in following. Posts are only permitted by those authorized by the public figure. Group pages are created to discuss a topic of interest to a group of people. This can be a person, company, product,

CyberLife

professional group, family or friends. All members of the group can and are encouraged to participate in the discussion.

CyberLife

Blogs

Blogs are online journals posted for public or restricted viewing. There are many applications and web hosting sites, which provide blogging functionality. Anyone can create a blog using one of the free blogging tools. To get started, create an account, set up your page layout and start writing. By selecting the page defaults, you can be writing your first blog post in just a few minutes.

Two of the most popular blogging sites are Wordpress (www.wordpress.com) and Blogger (www.blogger.com). Website domain hosting often includes blogging tools so your blog can be a part of your website, increasing your search engine optimization. Search engines like blogs because they are frequently updated with new content.

CyberLife™

You can blog about any topic you are interested in. The topics of your blog can enhance your career by demonstrating knowledge and expertise in your field. Your writing sets you apart as an expert. Each post is a stand alone entry though ideas can be continued or elaborated on in related posts. Blog postings can be as short as a few sentences or much longer if you choose. To build a consistent readership, plan on blogging once every week or two at a minimum.

Blogs can include text only or include other elements for interest, clarity and readability. Photographs, clip art, video and audio can be part of each of these posts. A picture is worth a thousand words and can convey your message more effectively. An embedded movie can emphasize and clarify your point. YouTube is a resource for free videos.

CyberLife

Include relevant keywords in your posts so others can find your content. Keywords are the words others would enter into a search engine like Google to find your content. Most blogging tools include a keyword section where you can enter a list of the relevant keywords making your content easier to find by readers.

CyberLife

YouTube

YouTube (www.youtube.com) is an online video sharing community. Anyone can watch videos on the site and members upload videos for others to watch. You can find videos on just about any subject on YouTube. YouTube is the second most popular search engine after Google.

When posting videos, use keywords to help others easily find your content. Videos can be organized in a channel or playlists for convenient viewing. By grouping related videos into a playlist, you can post or send a link to this group of videos rather than multiple links for each individual item.

If a picture is worth a thousand words, a video is worth a million or more. Popular videos are interesting, educational or both. There are unlimited ways to use YouTube creatively to boost

CyberLife

your career. Use keywords to find videos related to topics you are interested in researching. Open a free account and post your own videos on YouTube, create channels and playlists.

Your YouTube channel is a landing page or website address where you can direct others to view a list of all of your YouTube content. A playlist is a group of videos on a related topic. Watch my YouTube playlist of videos on my professional speaking at http://bit.ly/April_Speaks.

You can create an online resume for potential hiring managers to watch. Capture live shots of you demonstrating what you do best. Show off your unique selling proposition so others know why you are the best at what you do.

Show a potential customer how your product works by recording a demonstration and posting the video

CyberLife

online. Show off products for sale by recording clips and adding audio descriptions. Include keywords in the description when you post the videos so others will find them when searching YouTube.

CyberLife

Email

Email is not a social networking tool, though you can leverage its features to help you grow your online social network and visibility. Update your email signature to include your contact information and links to your social networking site profiles. Your phone number is another key piece of information to include within your signature.

Usually your email signature is updated within your email account settings. By adding these links to the bottom of each of the emails you send, the receiver is more inclined to visit your online profiles or give you a call. The easier you make it for others to contact you, the more likely they are to do so.

CyberLife™

Google

Google (www.google.com) aggregates information on the internet and is by far the most popular of search engines. You can search for your name using Google to be aware of what others may see when they do research on you. When you review these results, think of how a hiring manager or client may consider what they see.

A viewer would expect a professional established in their career to have a number of online references. If you have no online search results, people will wonder what you have contributed to your profession. Search results could also return information on other people with the same name who are not you. How will others know which results reference you or someone else? This is especially critical if the other person's references are negative. By differentiating yourself with a

P a g e | **33**

CyberLife

unique brand you can stand out from others and
avoid this confusion.

Set up alerts to let you know when Google has
found and indexed a reference to your name. Set up
your alerts at Google (www.google.com/alerts).
Enter your name in quotes to narrow this list to
the most relevant results. If you use nicknames or
other variations of your name, set alerts for these
terms as well. Consider adding alerts for your
company name, key products and competitors.

Which Tool?

Choose your social networking tools based on your desired results. There are different ways to make the most out of these social networking tools depending on your current career stage. As you shift from one career phase to another, you will want to evaluate your choice of tools and how you are using them.

CyberLife

Your Career Stage Today

You can use social networking tools differently as you move through different stages of your career. Each section below discusses the ways you can leverage these tools to maximize your results and minimize your investment of precious time.

CyberLife

High school student:

- You are likely using social networking tools like Facebook and MySpace (www.myspace.com) to connect with your friends. As you begin to consider a career, think about how future employers may evaluate you based on your online presence. Hiring managers regularly research candidates on social networking sites. If they find unprofessional messages, pictures and videos, you may be eliminated as a job candidate.

- A hiring manager may have different standards as to what is looked upon as unprofessional content. Consider asking school counselors or other trusted adults for their advice.

CyberLife

- Do we need to talk about sexting? Don't! Content on the internet lives forever.

- Take a good look at your social networking profiles from a hiring manager's perspective. It is time to make sure any photos, comments and links which could turn off an employer are removed. Tell your friends you are updating your page to project a more professional image and that you expect anything they post on your profile respects this. Monitor your profile to be sure it sends the right tone. Delete any content that could reflect poorly on you. When in doubt, choose the more conservative approach.

- Monitor your profile on these sites and immediately delete anything which could be considered negative by a hiring manager. Be

CyberLife

especially vigilant of comments and photos posted by others.

- Others will assume you are like those with whom you are connected to online. If you have friends or connections that are posting unprofessional comments, it is assumed that you will behave the same. It is said that birds of a feather, flock together. Consider this when choosing whom to connect with. Unfriend anyone who does not project an image you want associated with your professional presence.

CyberLife

College students:

- Full time and part time college students can use social networking tools to start building a professional network as they begin to explore careers. You may be active on Facebook and MySpace to connect with your friends. Now is the time to create a profile and build relationships on other tools geared towards professionals.

- LinkedIn is the first place to start creating professional connections. Create a profile in LinkedIn highlighting your college major, scholastic awards and interests. Create a link to presentations or papers you have written. Include community service and activities you participated in. For example, if you earned your Eagle Scout award, notate this in your profile. You want to include

CyberLife

items that may catch someone's attention
and start a conversation.

• Review all other social networking sites you
  previously used to be sure you consistently
  project a professional image. Employers and
  recruiters are checking Facebook, MySpace,
  Google and other sites to review your past. If
  there are party photos or comments you
  would not want your next employer to see,
  clean these up now. Google alerts can help
  you monitor your online profiles.

• Remember there is no such thing as
  "private" in the online world. While some
  social networking sites allow you to restrict
  access to parts of your profile, it is still very
  possible for others to gain access to
  information you post. It only takes a second
  to copy a file and save it to a hard drive or

P a g e | **41**

CyberLife™

other online site. Don't assume any private
information will remain private.

- Search LinkedIn groups for your college
name and join the alumni group. Listen in to
what is being discussed and join the
conversations. Contact those members who
currently work with employers of interest to
you. Now is the time to learn about the
culture of the company and find out about
corporate hiring practices.

- Highlight your accomplishments by posting
a YouTube video. Showcase research for a
class or thesis. Narrate a series of pictures
depicting something you built or created.

CyberLife

Employed in a service field:

- If you are a service provider, you can use these tools to highlight your capabilities. Ask your satisfied clients to post service provider recommendations on your LinkedIn profile. These third party endorsements from your customers are powerful sales tools.

- Build a community of people who are fans of your product or service by creating a Facebook Group page. Encourage discussion between your fans by asking questions or by soliciting feedback. Take photos of completed projects or works in progress and post these on your group page. Ask your client's permission first. Encourage others to post pictures of your work.

P a g e | **43**

CyberLife

- Create videos of you at work or show off completed projects and post these on YouTube. You can embed the video into your Facebook Group page or blog and encourage others to share their comments and experiences working with you.

- Create a YouTube playlist for a group of videos. A clothing designer could group business wear, formal wear, accessories or other like projects to show prospective clients finished work.

- Use Twitter to tweet updates about new services, incoming merchandise, special offers or news. Include links to photos and additional information.

CyberLife™

You are the hiring manager:

- When your company is ready to hire additional talent, use social networking sites to help you identify potential employees. Your pool of candidates you can reach expands with the number of connections you have. Build your own network to help you find the ideal person to fill your open position.

- LinkedIn is the number one hiring tool for most companies. You can purchase paid job postings on the site as well as post opportunities yourself.

- Post a message about the job opening in LinkedIn groups where members are likely candidates or know those who may be interested in learning more about the position.

P a g e | **45**

CyberLife

- Send a message to your LinkedIn contacts asking for referrals to those with appropriate qualifications. Ask your contacts to ask their contacts for candidates.

- Post the job opening on your website then use your status or update field in LinkedIn, Twitter and Facebook to notify others of the position. Include the job title and a link to the full job posting. Use a URL shortener if desired to keep the update within the 140 character limit restrictions.

- Use Twitter hashtags such as #jobs #careers to let others know you are posting job openings.

P a g e | **46**

CyberLife

- Use your Facebook Group page to let others know you are hiring. Your members may know candidates who are perfect for the job.

- By demonstrating cost effective hiring practices, you will be saving your company money and demonstrating your ability to find high quality candidates through a variety of channels. Your creativity could lead to a bonus for you.

CyberLife™

As a recruiter:

- Keep more of your commission by finding candidates through online sites. Active and passive job seekers await you on these social networking sites. The larger your network is, the more candidates available to you. Build a large network on LinkedIn, Facebook and Twitter.

- Post the full description of the job openings on your website or blog, then send a link to the detailed information through your LinkedIn, Facebook and Twitter status updates.

- When tweeting job postings, include the hashtag "#jobs" so others know you are sending a job posting related message. Other

CyberLife

hashtags such as #PM #security #insurance can describe the position further.

- Target LinkedIn groups where your candidates are likely to belong. For a process improvement specialist, seek out then join "Six Sigma" and "Lean" related groups and post your job opening there.

- Create a Facebook Group page to post all your job postings. Job seekers can browse the listings and contact you if they are interested in applying.

- Create videos of your candidates for hiring managers to view before the interview. Have the candidates introduce themselves and give their personal commercial showcasing how they can help their potential employer.

CyberLife

Advancing in your current job:

- In today's job market companies are eliminating staff in their organizations to reduce costs and improve organizational effectiveness. There are fewer jobs at the top of the organization and they are harder to land. To advance in your current position, your employer needs to see you as a leader in your company and in your industry.

- Create a profile on LinkedIn and highlight the industry related work you have done. Identify the keywords particular to your business and include them in your profile. Recognition from outside the organization adds credibility to your work.

- In your profile, talk about the results of your work including specific metrics and results you delivered. Document increased revenue and profit dollars you influenced. Note the percentage changes in customer satisfaction scores or other company metrics.

- Join industry related LinkedIn groups and take part in the conversation. Answer questions about your field or industry to demonstrate your expertise. Ask the opinions of your peers to keep up with what other companies are doing and to stay informed of changes in your field.

- Interestingly, when external organizations show they value you, your current employer will perceive you offer greater value to your own company. Note all industry papers you have written or presentations delivered with links to your online profiles or websites for additional information.

CyberLife

- Write LinkedIn recommendations for others who you worked with during your career. This includes customers, co-workers, managers, employees, vendors or partners. Often they will respond by writing a recommendation for you. As consumers, we value others opinions. Look at how Amazon uses product reviews to sell goods on its site.

- When you ask for recommendations from others, make it easy for them to comply. In your request, specify the achievements and skills you demonstrated and would like to have highlighted. This technique not only refreshes their memory, it makes their job easier to complete so they are more likely to comply with your request.

- Update your status on social networking sites regularly. Make a comment about a

P a g e | **52**

new business related book you are reading. Share links to industry papers you authored or read. Let others know when you make presentations on your topic. Frequent updates will keep your name in front of others and increase your visibility.

- Comment on articles posted in professional journals in your industry. Those in marketing or advertising could comment on a story in Advertising Age (www.adage.com). Become the "go-to" person when a media writer has a question or is looking for a quote by contacting your local newspaper business editor and offering your assistance.

- Read local newspapers and the Wall Street Journal. Send links to interesting articles to your network. Login to make comments and add your perspective to an article.

CyberLife

Looking for a lifestyle job:

- Just as that favorite pair of jeans from 10 years ago may not be a good fit for you today, your career may no longer fit your current needs. Early in our occupations we may have had the time, energy and desire to work long hours. Perhaps now you realize you would rather have more time to spend on your other passions. Maybe you are looking for a position with more flexibility. You are ready to be the worker bee rather than the queen bee.

- Now is the time to reframe your skills and qualifications to appeal to a different audience. Repackage yourself to let others know you have many skills to offer and not appear over qualified.

P a g e | **54**

CyberLife

- Use LinkedIn to create a profile that highlights your transferable skills and desired next role. Use this tool to broadcast your value proposition. De-emphasize your previous job titles by focusing on the results you accomplished.

- Build a strong network including those who are likely hiring managers or who may be connected to hiring managers. Keep up a dialog with your contacts to highlight your skills and how you can help an organization. Let them know your professional goals so they can be your advocates in your job search.

- Identify companies where you would like to work. Monitor job postings on LinkedIn and your target company's website. Develop contacts within the company and inquire about employee referral programs. Ask your contacts if they are willing to submit your resume to their employer. They may even be able to identify the hiring manager and deliver your resume directly to the manager's inbox or hands.

- People hire people they like. Build a large network and keep in contact with them regularly. As you interact with others, your best qualities will naturally show. People will remember this when jobs open up. Create a team of personal evangelists who are working for you.

- Volunteer for causes you are passionate about. Leverage your skills to benefit the organization and demonstrate your abilities. A fashion designer could design and make costumes for a theater production. A

CyberLife

musician could play for a charity night. A project manager could chair a special event. While you execute your role, others will see the quality of your work and are more likely to be your cheerleader.

CyberLife™

Your next career step is unclear:

- You may be at a crossroads in your career where you are just not sure what your next step is. Maybe you feel bored or unfulfilled in your current job. Perhaps your field is shrinking and you know it is time to move on to a growing industry. If you find yourself here, it is time for career exploration. Think back to the roles and activities that you most enjoyed in the past. Identify other roles which have those same elements. Note the titles and companies on your contacts profiles for ideas of where you may want to investigate in the future.

- Before jumping into a new field, learn more about what it may be like to work in this new environment by interviewing those who currently work in the industry. Ask contacts

CyberLife

if they would be willing to spend 15 or 30 minutes discussing how they got started in their career, skills required in their job or biggest challenges in their workday. These informational interviews are a method to gain insight and narrow down your choices.

- Use tools like LinkedIn and Twitter to search for keywords related to your field or skills. Check out the profiles of those who appear in the search results. Read their profiles and updates to see if this career choice resonates with you. If it looks interesting, contact the person to learn more about what they do. Most people are willing to share insights if you approach them in a non-threatening way. Be honest and upfront in your request. Tell them you are curious about their industry or role and would like to learn more. Ask for a 15 minute phone

CyberLife

conversation and include the questions you would like to ask. These informational interviews are valuable for learning about a typical day for someone in that career.

- Find a variety of people in roles of interest for a holistic view of the position. The beauty of social networking tools is you can find people all over the world. Depending on your specific field, you may contact people anywhere on the planet for information about a topic. Due to the competitive nature of some fields, people from outside your geographic area may be more likely to speak candidly with you and more willing to answer your questions.

CyberLife

Professional services:

- Professionals like lawyers, accountants and real estate agents live on referral business. When a prospective client needs these services, they are likely to ask their network for a recommendation. People recommend those they have had good relationships with and who are top of mind. To be the one your contacts will recommend, make a point of regularly reaching out to your network with valuable content. These communications also establish you as an expert in your field. For example, an accountant could send an article about upcoming tax law changes and the impact to small business owners. Realtors can communicate new homebuyer incentives.

P a g e | **61**

CyberLife

- Referrals are third party endorsements of your work and can make the sale for you. If a prospect is finding you through a reference, they are considering the personal recommendation a validation of your work. Proudly displaying recommendations on your LinkedIn profile and website from satisfied customers will make your prospective client more comfortable working with you. Encourage your customers and partners to post recommendations. You can sent a request through LinkedIn and include specific areas you would like them to comment on. This helps direct the feedback and highlight the areas important to you.

- Clients who use your services are likely to know others who can also use your services. Ask your current clients for referrals. Social networking tools make it easy to enable

CyberLife™

connections between your contacts. If a
client does refer a prospect to you, take the
time to say thank you and let them know
their efforts are appreciated.

- If you do pro bono work for local causes
  whether in your field or not, highlight this
  on your profile. Others will look for a way to
  connect with you and a favorite charity may
  be just the thing to spark interest in your
  profile. Use keywords in your description of
  your efforts so your work will show up in
  search results.

- Use your profile status updates to keep in
  communication with your network. Post
  positive client feedback on your profile. Let
  others know about work you just completed.
  Send links to topical information related to
  your industry. Write articles and

CyberLife

newsletters then send links to the online version of the article through your online status updates.

- Post links to articles written about you or by you on your website.

CyberLife

Self employed:

- As a self employed person, you are continually in a selling cycle. Whether you are currently working on a project or not, you have to be thinking just over the horizon to where your next sale will be. Let your social networking profile do the work for you.

- Use the status update feature in LinkedIn, Facebook and Twitter to let others know what you are doing. Always keep a positive tone to your statements. You can talk about learning something new, helping a client or completing a project. Send out an update about a special offer to drive revenue when business is slow. Here is a sample: "10% off new customer services. Good through this Thursday noon. Mention code #57."

CyberLife™

- Use industry keywords in your profile so others will find you in search results. Research other related words used when searching to find someone with your skills and services. Keyword density matters so use the most important words several times within your profile.

- Join online groups whose members are likely to benefit from your services or know others who would be interested. Accountants could join a local legal group to build connections with attorneys. Develop a relationship and establish yourself as a credible expert.

- Ask for recommendations from your satisfied clients. Third party endorsements are powerful sales tools. Use the LinkedIn request recommendations feature to prompt comments on a specific aspect of your work and skills.

- Use blogs, LinkedIn questions and YouTube to comment on your field and establish yourself as a thought leader in your industry. Share your perspective on where you see your professional world heading.

- Read industry specific journals and post online comments adding to the conversation on topics within your expertise. This builds your credibility in your field.

- Write a blog to demonstrate your industry knowledge and helpful content. Comments between you and your readers build a community around your subject matter.

CyberLife

- Encourage customers to post testimonials on your blog about how satisfied they were with your services. The can post pictures of themselves using or benefiting from your service.

P a g e | **68**

CyberLife

Contract work:

- Some professionals prefer the independence of contract work. If you are one of the many people who have been laid off recently, you may be using contract work to bring in temporary income. Help others help you find your next job by letting them know you are open to new opportunities. Use your social networking profile to show the type of work you are looking for and your ideal industry.

- Use your network to learn more about local companies where you might like to work. Make an internal connection and ask the person to meet for coffee or a phone conversation. You will be better able to determine if the company is a fit for you and your values. Your contact will learn about you and therefore be better able to represent

CyberLife

you for a future opening at this company or introduce you to another person.

- Find out if this is one of the many companies that have employee referral programs. Ask your contact if this company has a program and if they are willing to refer you. The employee will often benefit financially if you are hired.

- Join affinity groups related to your target companies. Many current and former employees have created LinkedIn groups to communicate with their peers. By joining these groups you can listen in on the conversation to better understand the current corporate environment and culture. Ask group members questions about the company, current projects and priorities.

CyberLife

Staying in the know:

- Social networking tools are perfect for keeping in the know. There is no longer a "news hour" where broadcasters tell us what happened over the past day. If you want to stay in the know, just check out your favorite social networking site and listen in to the conversation.

- One of my favorite places to keep up with the news in the world is the trending topics section of Twitter's home page. You can immediately see what others are interested in and talking about right now. You can select to see worldwide trends or a localized version.

- Social networking members talk about what is happening now. Just log in to Facebook or

LinkedIn and read the latest status updates to find out about the current trending topics. You will read about everything from world politics to local incidents in seconds. News moves faster now that we have adopted social networking tools.

- If you're someone who has trouble making small talk at networking events and parties, here is a tip for you. Check out the hot trends on the social networking sites your fellow attendees are using to find out what is news right now. You will be prepared to answer questions or start a conversation by having background on a variety of topics.

- Learn from your peers in your industry. Search Technorati (www.technorati.com) for the hottest blog topics. This is a great way to stay up on the latest trends in your field.

CyberLife

Search for keywords to see what turns up.
You don't need to read all the postings. Just
get a feel for the topics currently discussed
and why they are important to your field.

You hate the thought of social networking:

- I know some people cringe when they hear others talking about social networking. They may even roll their eyes and sigh. While no one is required to use social networking tools, it is important to know how they are used and why they are so popular. Also important is a knowledge of what you are missing by not participating on these sites. Once the facts are understood, an educated decision can be made.

- Recruiters and hiring managers are pressed to keep recruiting costs down. They find a plethora of high quality candidates available to them just by searching Google and LinkedIn. Currently, 80% of all companies use LinkedIn as their primary recruiting tool. It does not make sense for companies to

CyberLife™

spend hundreds or even thousands of dollars to post a position on job boards when they can search online sites and find the right candidates for free.

- These hiring managers and recruiters have found an even easier way to fill open positions. Companies and recruiters are using social networking sites to post job openings. Using this technique, candidates come directly to the person who posts the opportunity with no middleman to collect a fee.

- If you are not on social networking sites, you are missing hot leads and job postings as they become available. Also, it is much harder for others to forward you a job lead from one site to another. If it is too much work to forward the information to a

CyberLife

different social networking site, they may give up and you will lose the opportunity to learn about what could have been the ideal job for you.

- While you may hate social networking, the reality is if you are not using these sites, hiring managers will see you as out of touch. You will seem backward, behind the times and unfamiliar with current trends. The benefit of joining social networking sites to boost your professional career is priceless.

- Take the plunge and spend an hour creating a LinkedIn profile. Go in once a week and update your status to highlight something positive in your professional life. A few minutes a week is a small investment to give you a presence online.

CyberLife

You use social networking site for fun, not for your career:

- The reason why Facebook has over 400 million active users is because members have fun interacting with each other. There is nothing wrong with using a social networking site to virtually hang out with your friends. You can also use these sites to enhance your professional life.

- Some sites allow you to restrict access to parts of your profile to friends or connections. Even though you can shield information, do not be lulled into a false sense of security. Assume anything that is posted online can and will get out. With a simple right click, a picture can be copied then saved to someone's computer hard drive where the evidence can be archived

CyberLife

forever. The photo can be attached to an email or posted on other social networking sites with a click of a button. Don't be surprised by pictures of you showing up unexpectedly. If you would be uncomfortable to see a particular photo of yourself on the cover of the New York Times, don't post it online. If other people post pictures you would prefer not to see online, contact them and request the offending picture be taken down immediately.

- Consider joining social networking sites with an eye on building connections with other professionals in your field. Seek out those who are in related or complementary fields. As a career coach, I connect with recruiters who are looking for candidates to fill job openings.

CyberLife™

- Keep your updates professional in nature. You can still have fun and enjoy your time networking online with friends. Before you post a comment or picture, think about how other professionals will view your updates.

CyberLife

Targeting a specific industry or company:

- During your career, you may learn about a company or industry which appeals to you. Maybe your internal compass compels you to be aligned to a passion like the "green" industry. Perhaps you want to work for a company that solves a specific problem for people like Habitat for Humanity. Search Twitter for others in your target industry or company. Twitter Search (Search.twitter.com) is the tool for searching all Twitter posts for keywords. Tweets are also indexed by search engines Google and Bing for increased search results.

- Search LinkedIn groups for an affinity group based on your area of interest. Members are self selected based on skills, interests, industries, professions and geography.

CyberLife

Larger groups provide a bigger pool of people to learn from. Join up to 50 different LinkedIn groups and listen to the conversation. Groups with a global membership provide a wide perspective and insights to the group. Consider groups in your local area to combine in person and online networking.

- Once you find others talking about your subject of interest, reach out to them privately and engage them in dialog. Ask specific questions to gather information about your topic or links to additional resources.

Social Networking
Throughout Your Career

CyberLife

You are in a declining industry or company:

- As our society evolves, our need for products and services also change. If you find the products and services your company offers are no longer relevant to the market, it is time to find a more stable or growing industry. Social networking tools can help you do just that. Use the search functionality to find industries or people in your area who work for growing market segments. Contact them directly or through a common connection to learn more.

- Highlight your transferable skills in your status updates. Almost all roles require leadership, time management, organization and team skills. Let others know you have created a strategic plan, successfully facilitated a meeting or negotiated a deal.

CyberLife

- Show evidence that you are growing your skills through continuous development. If you are not growing, you are growing stale. Focus on re-educating yourself. Brush up on the soft skills important in any job. Update your status when you take a class, attend a seminar or write an industry paper.

- Check out the U.S. Bureau of Labor Statistics (www.bls.gov) to learn about growing fields and job titles. Find out about education requirements, salary ranges and industry news. Once you narrow your interests to few areas, reach out to those in your network to identify contacts in these specific industries. Get perspectives on what a typical day is really like. Ask for referral to others so you can get a broader viewpoint.

P a g e | **83**

CyberLife

Change careers:

- Finding a new job in the same job function and same industry is hard enough in today's economy. Changing either job function or industry makes the job search that much more difficult. Changing both your industry and function is the hardest job change. Difficult. Yes. Impossible? No.

- Talk to others who have made dramatic shifts in their careers. I recently met a former nuclear weapons programmer who now manages large information technology systems for the company in medical industry. I have personally shifted both roles and industries in a single job change. This situation is not as uncommon as you may think.

CyberLife

- Highlight your transferable skills by focusing on the big picture rather than the details. Accomplishments like redesigning a process or building a team from scratch are valuable to all industries.

- Build a network of people who know your skills and desired future role. Be a contributor to the conversation and demonstrate your expertise. Let them be your advocates with their eyes and ears seeking out new opportunities for you. Keep them updated about your progress.

- Find groups on LinkedIn relating to your new career. Get to know others and find out the types of skills most valued in the field or company. Ask for information on companies who are expanding their offerings or locations.

P a g e | **85**

CyberLife

Portfolio careers:

- Our economy is changing which in turn affects hiring practices. It is more common to take on contract and part-time work. Workers may combine working for others while running their own business. With a portfolio career, income comes in from multiple sources rather than a single full-time employment situation. Freelance work may be combined with part-time employment. Seasonal sales may provide supplemental income.

- By combining income from various streams of work, you are better able to withstand market place changes or layoffs. As we continue to change our work practices, portfolio careers will become more commonplace.

P a g e | **86**

CyberLife

- Use social networking tools to highlight the common skills and traits that you use in all facets of your portfolio career. Project management, event planning and relationship building are commonly needed skill for most job titles

- Market specific types of work at different times by updating your profiles on each of the sites. If you own an accounting business you could highlight tax preparation in the spring, monthly accounting services in the summer, reducing tax liability in the fall and long term planning in the winter.

CyberLife

Semi retired:

- After a long career, you may be ready to take it easy and spend more time doing leisure activities but not be ready to completely leave the work force. Financial constraints or health insurance needs could require you to remain employed. Use your social networking as a way to keep yourself visible to your peers so they know you are actively employed or looking for a new job.

- Social networking sites are often used by hiring managers to post part-time positions. Monitor social networking sites and respond quickly if you see a position of interest.

- Let your peers know the type of work you are interested in so they can help you find

CyberLife

the ideal position. They are extra eyes and
ears working for you.

- Update your status on these sites to let
  others know what you are doing. This keeps
  you top of mind for others and lets them
  know you are staying active.

CyberLife

Retired:

- Social networking brings all people together. Stay in touch with your friends and former co-workers through one-to-one relationships, alumni groups and special interest groups. Search LinkedIn and Facebook for the names of former employers to find groups where you can mingle with other current or past employees.

- If your search for a group to join on a social networking site does not identify the group you are looking for, start your own group. When you set up a Facebook group page or LinkedIn group, you choose the attributes important to you. Membership can be open to the public or be private. Group content can be restricted to the group or viewable by the general public. I created a group in 2000

CyberLife

that is still actively used today to keep in touch with former co-workers and share job leads. There is even an annual holiday event to bring everyone together in person.

- Your goals and desires may change over the years and maintaining a network will help you if you desire to return to work or consider contract work. A short-term project could fit in with your schedule and provide income for a few indulgences in your life.

CyberLife

You do not have time for social networking:

- Social networking does take time. Only you can determine if the benefits you will receive outweigh the time investment. Communications and relationships are evolving. By ignoring the tools others are using, you are left out of the conversation. As the popularity of social networking continues to grow, the value of participating will increase proportionally.

- What has worked for you so far in your career may not get you where you want to go now or in the future. As scarce as good jobs are, it does not make sense to turn away from so many opportunities.

- Consider taking a small step and creating a profile on one of the social networking sites. To help you decide which site to choose, ask

your peers or others you know professionally
which tools they use. Select the one most
commonly used by your contacts.

- Create your profile including all the
information you are interested in sharing.
Ask your peers to check out your profile and
give you feedback. Use their comments to
improve your profile.

- Return to your social networking site on a
regular schedule and notice the changes.
Depending on the tool you chose, check your
inbox for email, reply to comments and
update your status.

- After using this tool for a while, ask yourself
what value it added to your professional
career. If you noticed a difference, consider

CyberLife

expanding to additional social networking
sites.

- Make a point of visiting these sites are a
regular interval to continue the conversation
with your network.

CyberLife™

Conclusion

While tools may change over the course of time, the basic principles remain the same. Getting a job is all about networking and networking is all about relationships.

It is not who you know. It is who you know knows.

Social networking tools enable information to move faster and spread wider. These tools do not replace the telephone and in person meetings. Instead they augment and deepen the relationship you build with others.

As your career evolves, so will your use of social networking tools. These sites can benefit your career in different ways as you migrate through your professional life.

For more career and networking tips, check out our blog at: http://www.cyberlifetutors.com/blog

CyberLife

Glossary of Terms

Affinity Group – A group connected together by a common interest or issue.

Bing – (www.bing.com) A search engine owned by Microsoft. Bing indexes and displays Twitter tweets within search results.

Blog – An online journal or diary.

Blogger – One who writes a blog.

Blogging – The act of writing a blog posting.

Channel – A customizable YouTube webpage with the member's profile, posted videos and other information.

Connection – A person who is connected to other through a network.

Demographics – The characteristics of a population.

CyberLife

Facebook – (www.facebook.com) A popular multimedia social networking site.

Farmville – An interactive, online game popular with Facebook users.

Google – (www.google.com) A search engine owned by Microsoft. Bing indexes and displays Twitter tweets within search results.

Hashtag – The pound symbol (#) used with keywords to aggregate topics for searching Twitter content. Examples: #Chicago, #jobs, #careers, #Insurance, #news.

Inbound link – A hyperlink from one website referring to an address or another website.

Keywords - Words used by web sites to search and index information.

Landing page – A URL or webpage to direct website visitors.

Lean – A quality improvement process.

LinkedIn – A social networking sites popular with professionals.

Mafia Wars – An interactive, online game popular with Facebook users.

Natural search results – The results which appear in search engine pages based on the content of the webpage.

Network – A group of people connected to each other directly or through an intermediary.

Paid search results – Results which appear on search engine pages as a result of paid advertisements.

Playlist – A way of organizing list of music or videos on YouTube.

Portfolio career – A variety of different activities which combined produce annual income.

CyberLife

Profile – Information on a social networking site created by and about a member.

Retweet: To rebroadcast another Twitter user's message to your Twitter followers.

Search engine optimization (SEO) - A process of improving traffic to a website through natural search results.

Search terms – Words or phases entered into search engines to find specific content.

Sexting – To send sexually explicit text, photographs or video through computers or mobile devices.

Six Sigma - A process to improve quality.

Social network – An network of people and communities connected to on another. Online social networks connect people through internet based tool.

CyberLife

Trending topics – A list of the most common recently tweeted Twitter terms.

Twitter – (www.twitter.com) A social networking tool based on 140 character micro messages.

URL Shorteners – Websites which convert a webpage address or URL to an address with fewer characters and/or a memorable name. Two sites I use are Bit.ly (http://bit.ly) and TinyURL (http://tinyurl.com).

Viral – To spread rapidly from one person to another through the internet as a illness might spread from person to person.

YouTube – (www.youtube.com) A video sharing site.

About the Author

April M. Williams is a nationally recognized speaker, author and coach who has assisted hundreds of people in career transition. By demonstrating the power of social networking tools, April shows clients how to leverage their strengths to enhance their careers. April has published books and numerous articles on career building as well as other related business topics. She has been featured in major publications including the Wall Street Journal, Project Management Institute, Savvy and Nations Restaurant News. April is a contributing editor to the Hawaii travel website 808Talk (www.808talk.com).

An entrepreneur, April is President of CyberLife Tutors (www.cyberlifetutors.com). She has also been recognized as a Project Management Professional (PMP) by the Project Management

CyberLife

Institute. She has demonstrated knowledge and skill in leading and directing project teams. This requires delivering project results within the constraints of schedule, budget and resources. April earned her Master's Degree (Information Systems) and Bachelor's (Telecommunications) from Roosevelt University, Schaumburg, Illinois.

Prior to launching her speaking, writing and coaching career, April led technical projects and programs for Fortune 50 companies. Her career has included creating alignment across organizational boundaries and building consensus among people with multiple agendas. April has transformed her skills in working with people, processes and technology to leverage social media and personal marketing for career and business development. She is a career advisor at the Barrington Career Center and an Executive on the

CyberLife

Chicago Women in Technology International (www.witi.com) network.

April's personal marketing, project organization and job search programs offer audiences practical business strategies and insight that can produce profitable bottom-line results.

April is available for speaking engagements for corporations, associations, public seminars and events, and industry-specific trainings. See what people are saying about April's presentations by watching her April Speaks (http://bit.ly/April_Speaks) playlist on YouTube. For booking information call 847-207-7412. Entrepreneur, small business and career coaching available. Visit www.CyberLifeTutors.com or email April@CyberLifeTutors.com for more information.

P a g e | **104**

CyberLife™

Connect with April Online:

LinkedIn
http://www.LinkedIn.com/in/AprilMWilliams

Twitter
http://www.twitter.com/AprilMWilliams

Facebook
http://www.facebook.com/aprilmwilliams

YouTube
http://www.youtube.com/AprilMWilliams

Where's April Blog
http://aprilmwilliams.wordpress.com

Career and Networking Blog
http://www.cyberlifetutors.com/blog

Cyberlife Tutors Website
http://www.cyberlifetutors.com

Notes Page

CyberLife

Notes Page

Notes Page

www.ingramcontent.com/pod-product-compliance
Lightning Source LLC
Chambersburg PA
CBHW060626210326
41520CB00010B/1487